11/16/16
19.99

For M., herself a quote.

And to the brilliant minds quoted throughout this book.
Wish I had said it first.

... HE WRAPPED
HIMSELF IN QUOTATIONS—
AS A BEGGAR WOULD
ENFOLD HIMSELF IN THE
PURPLE OF EMPERORS.

RUDYARD KIPLING

INTRODUCTION

In my life, I have been a writer, a magazine and book editor, a photographer, a teenage website developer, a bad graphic designer, a four-chord musician, and even an aspiring barista/poet (for eight hours, anyway, until I realized I'd much rather be browsing the shelves of the bookstore that housed the coffee shop).

As all creatives know, the struggle is real. Committing acts of creativity—no matter the pursuit, no matter the discipline—is not easy (and can be downright hellish, depending on the day).

In other words, not all of us have it as good as writer Ray Bradbury, who cheerfully quipped, "I don't need an alarm clock—my ideas wake me."

Most of us are, perhaps, a bit more in poet Henry Wadsworth Longfellow's camp—"Art is long, and time is fleeting"—or maybe even actor Christopher Parker's: "Procrastination is like a credit card—it's a lot of fun until you get the bill."

Over the years, through creative blocks in between writing books and thousands of articles, shooting photos and editing magazine issues, through countless hours staring into the taunting white snow of blank screens, I've had a secret weapon to keep me moving forward, plodding on, sane—and it wasn't a library of self-help books or the attention of a gaggle of snake-oil-sellin' creative healers.

Rather, it was, simply enough, a Word file in which I collected (read: hoarded) quotes. A mainline of wisdom from the creative heroes who have inspired and informed so many of us.

To me, a good quote is the equivalent of a poem, or perhaps the occasional sip (read: pint) of good bourbon—a poultice for the creative soul. Such tiny, perfect revelations.

A good quote can humor. It can engage. It can enrage. It can inspire. It can motivate, and a simple sentence has been known to spawn an entire universe entirely of one's own.

This volume is meant for writers. For designers. For artists. For architects, poets, journalists, the dreamers, the believers—anyone with the creative urge haunting the depths of their bones.

Quotes float around the heart of that urge like fireflies, revealing, in their own way, a mosaic of what it means to be a creative, what it means to share a universal calling and gift that so many of us will not (and cannot) turn our backs on.

As designer Saul Bass said, "Interesting things happen when the creative impulse is cultivated with curiosity, freedom and intensity."

It is my hope that this book may just help foster the seeds of that intensity.

—Zachary Petit, Cincinnati, 2016

The real giants have always been poets, men who jumped from facts into the realm of imagination and ideas.

BILL BERNBACH

WHATEVER YOU'RE MEANT
TO DO, DO IT NOW. THE
CONDITIONS ARE ALWAYS
IMPOSSIBLE.

DORIS LESSING

ONLY HE WHO ATTEMPTS
THE ABSURD IS CAPABLE
OF ACHIEVING THE
IMPOSSIBLE.

MIGUEL DE UNAMUNO

If I am not mistaken, the words "art" and "artist" did not exist during the Renaissance and before: there were simply architects, sculptors, and painters, practicing a trade.

M.C. ESCHER

I FIND OUT WHAT THE WORLD NEEDS. THEN I GO AHEAD AND TRY TO INVENT IT.

THOMAS EDISON

KEEP A SMALL CAN
OF WD-40 ON YOUR
DESK—AWAY FROM
ANY OPEN FLAMES—
TO REMIND YOURSELF
THAT IF YOU DON'T
WRITE DAILY, YOU
WILL GET RUSTY.

GEORGE SINGLETON

DO NOT HOARD WHAT
SEEMS GOOD FOR A LATER
PLACE IN THE BOOK,
OR FOR ANOTHER BOOK;
GIVE IT,
GIVE IT ALL,
GIVE IT NOW.

ANNIE DILLARD

EVERYONE HAS TALENT.
WHAT IS RARE IS THE
COURAGE TO FOLLOW THE
TALENT TO THE DARK PLACES
WHERE IT LEADS.

ERICA JONG

Don't waste
time learning
the "tricks of
the trade."

Instead,
learn the trade.

H. JACKSON BROWN, JR.

Creativity is the world's greatest weapon. It always wins.

MIMI VALDÉS

We have art
in order not
to die of
the truth.

FRIEDRICH NIETZSCHE

The first step—especially for young people with energy and drive and talent, but not money—the first step to controlling your world is to control your culture. To model and demonstrate the kind of world you demand to live in. To write the books. Make the music. Shoot the films. Paint the art.

CHUCK PALAHNIUK

INTERESTING THINGS
HAPPEN WHEN THE
CREATIVE IMPULSE
IS CULTIVATED WITH
CURIOSITY, FREEDOM,
AND INTENSITY.

SAUL BASS

"WHEN I WAS A CHILD, ADULTS WOULD TELL ME NOT TO MAKE THINGS UP, WARNING ME OF WHAT WOULD HAPPEN IF I DID. AS FAR AS I CAN TELL SO FAR IT SEEMS TO INVOLVE LOTS OF FOREIGN TRAVEL AND NOT HAVING TO GET UP TOO EARLY IN THE MORNING."

NEIL GAIMAN

I didn't really know how I was going to make money creating art, but I knew I was going to make it.

JESSICA HISCHE

SOME ARE BORN GREAT, SOME
ACHIEVE GREATNESS, AND
SOME HAVE GREATNESS THRUST
UPON 'EM.

WILLIAM SHAKESPEARE

SOME MEN ARE BORN
MEDIOCRE, SOME MEN
ACHIEVE MEDIOCRITY, AND
SOME MEN HAVE MEDIOCRITY
THRUST UPON THEM.

JOSEPH HELLER

I saw that
my life was a
vast glowing
empty page
and I could
do anything
I wanted.

JACK KEROUAC

GENIUS IS ONLY A
GREATER APTITUDE
TO PATIENCE.

GEORGES-LOUIS LECLERC,
COMTE DE BUFFON

IDEAS ARE LIKE RABBITS.

YOU GET A COUPLE AND
LEARN HOW TO HANDLE THEM,
AND PRETTY SOON YOU HAVE
A DOZEN.

JOHN STEINBECK

Be willing
to get fired
for a good
idea.

SPIKE JONZE

That's the
great secret
of creativity.
You treat ideas
like cats:
You make them
follow you.

RAY BRADBURY

DON'T WORRY ABOUT PEOPLE
STEALING YOUR IDEAS. IF
YOUR IDEAS ARE ANY GOOD,
YOU'LL HAVE TO RAM THEM
DOWN PEOPLE'S THROATS.

HOWARD H. AIKEN

BUT THE TRUTH IS, IT'S NOT THE IDEA, IT'S NEVER THE IDEA, IT'S ALWAYS WHAT YOU DO WITH IT.

NEIL GAIMAN

ART IS A SORT OF
EXPERIMENTAL STATION IN
WHICH ONE TRIES OUT LIVING.

JOHN CAGE

The things that made you weird as a kid make you great as an adult— but only if you pay attention to them.

JAMES VICTORE

"THE DIFFERENCE
BETWEEN THE ALMOST
RIGHT WORD AND THE
RIGHT WORD IS REALLY
A LARGE MATTER—
'TIS THE DIFFERENCE
BETWEEN THE LIGHTNING-
BUG AND THE LIGHTNING."

MARK TWAIN

If you do it right, it will last

forever.

MASSIMO VIGNELLI

IT IS BETTER TO FAIL
IN ORIGINALITY THAN TO
SUCCEED IN IMITATION.

HERMAN MELVILLE

IMITATION CAN BE COMMERCIAL SUICIDE.

BILL BERNBACH

" I can't give you a surefire formula for success, but I can give you a formula for failure:

try to please everybody all the time. **"**

HERBERT BAYARD SWOPE

KNOW YOUR LITERARY TRADITION, SAVOR IT, STEAL FROM IT, BUT WHEN YOU SIT DOWN TO WRITE, FORGET ABOUT WORSHIPING GREATNESS AND FETISHIZING MASTERPIECES.

ALLEGRA GOODMAN

AN INTELLECTUAL IS A MAN
WHO SAYS A SIMPLE THING IN A
DIFFICULT WAY; AN ARTIST IS
A MAN WHO SAYS A DIFFICULT
THING IN A SIMPLE WAY.

CHARLES BUKOWSKI

Creativity is allowing
yourself to make mistakes.

Art is knowing which
ones to keep.

SCOTT ADAMS

The road to hell
is paved with
works-in-progress.

PHILIP ROTH

The road to hell is
paved with adverbs.

STEPHEN KING

" STYLE IS NOT NEUTRAL;
IT GIVES MORAL DIRECTIONS. "

MARTIN AMIS

Style is to forget all styles.

JULES RENARD

Art washes
away from the
soul the dust of
everyday life.

PABLO PICASSO

"A work of art works because it is true, not because it is real."

YANN MARTEL

WHEN FACING A
DIFFICULT TASK, ACT
AS THOUGH IT IS
IMPOSSIBLE TO FAIL.
IF YOU'RE GOING
AFTER MOBY DICK,
TAKE ALONG THE
TARTAR SAUCE.

H. JACKSON BROWN, JR.

You can't build a reputation on what you are going to do.

HENRY FORD

A poem . . .

begins as a lump in the throat,

a sense of wrong,

a homesickness,

a lovesickness.

ROBERT FROST

TO ME, THE GREATEST
PLEASURE OF WRITING
IS NOT WHAT IT'S ABOUT,
BUT THE INNER MUSIC
THAT WORDS MAKE.

TRUMAN CAPOTE

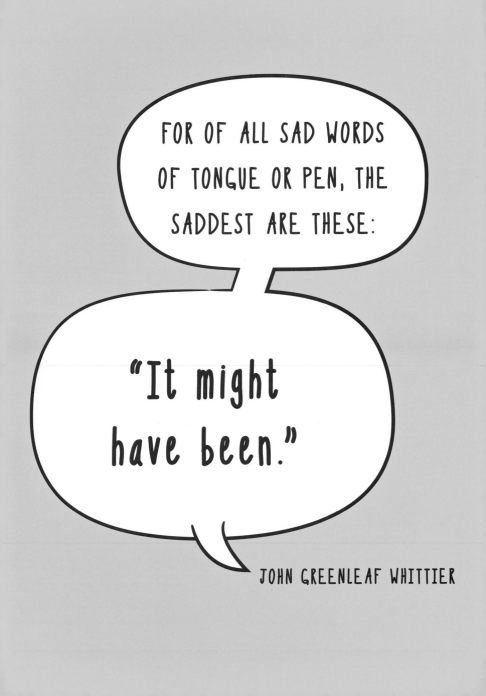

If a thing is worth having, it's worth cheating for.

W.C. FIELDS

They who dream by day are cognizant of many things which escape those who dream only by night.

EDGAR ALLAN POE

YOU MUST PUT INTO YOUR WORK
FIRST EFFORT, SECOND LOVE,
AND THIRD SUFFERING.

GLENN MURCUTT

NEVER FALL IN LOVE WITH AN IDEA. THEY'RE WHORES: IF THE ONE YOU'RE WITH ISN'T DOING THE JOB, THERE'S ALWAYS, ALWAYS, *ALWAYS* ANOTHER.

CHIP KIDD

PROCRASTINATION IS LIKE
A CREDIT CARD—IT'S A
LOT OF FUN UNTIL YOU
GET THE BILL.

CHRISTOPHER PARKER

ART IS LONG,
AND TIME IS FLEETING.

HENRY WADSWORTH LONGFELLOW

WALK ON AIR
AGAINST YOUR
BETTER JUDGEMENT.

SEAMUS HEANEY

Cheat your landlord if you can and must, but do not try to shortchange the Muse.

It cannot be done.

You can't fake quality any more than you can fake a good meal.

WILLIAM S. BURROUGHS

TIMES NEW ROMAN IS NOT A FONT
CHOICE SO MUCH AS THE ABSENCE OF
A FONT CHOICE, LIKE THE BLACKNESS
OF DEEP SPACE IS NOT A COLOR.

MATTHEW BUTTERICK

In a badly designed book, the letters mill and stand like starving horses in a field. . . . In a well-made book, where designer, compositor and printer have all done their jobs, no matter how many thousands of lines and pages, the letters are alive. They dance in their seats. Sometimes they rise and dance in the margins and aisles.

ROBERT BRINGHURST

Get in over your
head as often
and as joyfully
as possible.

ALEXANDER ISLEY

"ONE HAS TO BE BOTH CONSCIOUS AND UNCONSCIOUS AT THE SAME TIME. CLEAR THINKING AT THE WRONG MOMENT CAN STIFLE INSPIRATION AND TALENT."

KARL LAGERFELD

You have to
get bad
in order to
get good.

PAULA SCHER

" Everything
comes to him
who hustles
while he waits. "

THOMAS EDISON

I AM INTERESTED IN IMPERFECTIONS, QUIRKINESS, INSANITY, UNPREDICTABILITY. THAT'S WHAT WE REALLY PAY ATTENTION TO ANYWAY. WE DON'T TALK ABOUT PLANES FLYING; WE TALK ABOUT THEM CRASHING.

TIBOR KALMAN

PEOPLE SEEM TO THINK IF THEY
DRESS LIKE A REVOLUTIONARY
THEY DON'T ACTUALLY HAVE TO
BEHAVE LIKE ONE.

BANKSY

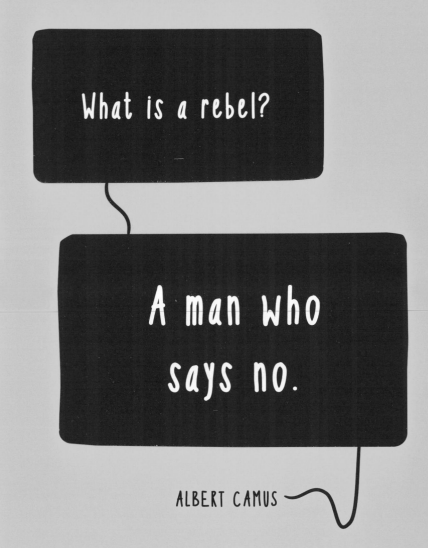

"The greatest
expression of
rebellion is joy."

JOSS WHEDON

THE FORMS SAID I'D BE A GOOD
ENGINEER. BUT THOSE DORKS JUST
DIDN'T SEEM TOO FUN TO HANG WITH,
SO I WENT AFTER ART AS A FOCUS.

AARON DRAPLIN

Wearing down seven
number-two pencils is
a good day's work.

ERNEST HEMINGWAY

Success is dangerous.

One begins to copy oneself,
and to copy oneself is more
dangerous than to copy others.

PABLO PICASSO

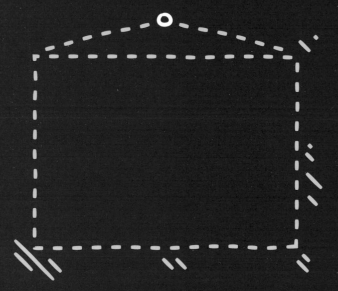

DON'T WORRY ABOUT PEOPLE STEALING YOUR
DESIGN WORK. WORRY ABOUT THE DAY THEY STOP.

JEFFREY ZELDMAN

AS SOON AS I BECAME
A LONER IN MY OWN
MIND, THAT'S WHEN I GOT
WHAT YOU MIGHT CALL A
"FOLLOWING." AS SOON
AS YOU STOP WANTING
SOMETHING YOU GET IT.

ANDY WARHOL

" IF A CLUTTERED DESK
IS A SIGN OF
A CLUTTERED MIND,
OF WHAT, THEN, IS
AN EMPTY DESK A SIGN? "

ALBERT EINSTEIN

Simplicity and complexity need each other.

JOHN MAEDA

IT SEEMS THAT PERFECTION
IS ATTAINED NOT WHEN THERE
IS NOTHING MORE TO ADD,
BUT WHEN THERE IS NOTHING
MORE TO TAKE AWAY.

ANTOINE DE SAINT-EXUPÉRY

FOLLOW YOUR INNER MOONLIGHT;
DON'T HIDE THE MADNESS.

ALLEN GINSBERG

Stop acting so small.
You are the universe
in ecstatic motion.

RUMI

" ONE MUST STILL
HAVE CHAOS
WITHIN ONESELF
TO GIVE BIRTH TO
A DANCING STAR. "

FRIEDRICH NIETZSCHE

Love is the axis and breath of my life. The art I produce is a byproduct, an excrescence of love, the song I sing, the joy which must explode, the overabundance—that is all!

ANAÏS NIN

I dream my
painting and then
I paint my dream.

VINCENT VAN GOGH

WRITING IS FLYING IN DREAMS. WHEN YOU REMEMBER. WHEN YOU CAN. WHEN IT WORKS. IT'S THAT EASY.

NEIL GAIMAN

I am not sure that I exist, actually. I am all the writers that I have read, all the people that I have met, all the women that I have loved; all the cities that I have visited, all my ancestors.

JORGE LUIS BORGES

WRITING IS PERHAPS
THE GREATEST OF
HUMAN INVENTIONS,
BINDING TOGETHER
PEOPLE, CITIZENS
OF DISTANT EPOCHS,
WHO NEVER KNEW ONE
ANOTHER. BOOKS BREAK
THE SHACKLES OF TIME,
PROOF THAT HUMANS CAN
WORK MAGIC.

CARL SAGAN

Practice

safe design:

Use a

concept.

PETRULA VRONTIKIS

" BY ALL MEANS BREAK THE RULES,
AND BREAK THEM BEAUTIFULLY,
DELIBERATELY, AND WELL.

THAT IS ONE OF THE ENDS
FOR WHICH THEY EXIST. "

ROBERT BRINGHURST

" It is important to have questionable friends you can trust unconditionally. **"**

CHUCK KLOSTERMAN

I always start writing
with a clean piece of
paper and a dirty mind.

PATRICK DENNIS

Writing is not necessarily something to be ashamed of, but do it in private and wash your hands afterwards.

ROBERT A. HEINLEIN

If you dig a hole and it's in the wrong place, digging it deeper isn't going to help.

SEYMOUR CHWAST

PUT YOUR DESK IN THE CORNER, AND
EVERY TIME YOU SIT DOWN THERE
TO WRITE, REMIND YOURSELF WHY IT
ISN'T IN THE MIDDLE OF THE ROOM.
LIFE ISN'T A SUPPORT-SYSTEM FOR
ART. IT'S THE OTHER WAY AROUND.

STEPHEN KING

TO GAIN YOUR OWN VOICE,

YOU HAVE TO FORGET

ABOUT HAVING IT HEARD.

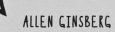

ALLEN GINSBERG

When I was a child
my mother said to me,
"If you become a soldier
you'll be a general.
If you become a monk
you'll end up as the Pope."
Instead I became a
painter and wound up
as Picasso.

PABLO PICASSO

I'M TOTALLY CRAZY, I
KNOW THAT. I DON'T SAY
THAT TO BE A SMARTASS,
BUT I KNOW THAT THAT'S
THE VERY ESSENCE OF
WHAT MAKES MY WORK
GOOD. AND I KNOW MY
WORK IS GOOD. NOT
EVERYBODY LIKES IT,
THAT'S FINE. I DON'T
DO IT FOR EVERYBODY.
OR ANYBODY. I DO IT
BECAUSE I CAN'T NOT
DO IT.

MAURICE SENDAK

Think of, and look at, your work as though it were done by your enemy. If you look at it to admire it you are lost.

SAMUEL BUTLER

YOU'LL NEVER GO
WRONG WHEN YOU
WORK WITH SOMEONE
SMARTER THAN YOU.

TIBOR KALMAN

"Sure, our competitors will laugh. Let them laugh so hard that they cannot breathe.

SAM WARD

WHEN YOU'RE LIVING IN THE
MOMENT, YOU'RE LIVING
IN THE MOMENT; WHATEVER
THAT MOMENT IS, THAT'S
YOUR REALITY. EVERYTHING
ELSE IS A MYTH.

STEVEN HELLER

My fate cannot be mastered; it can only be collaborated with and thereby, to some extent, directed. Nor am I the captain of my soul; I am only its noisiest passenger.

ALDOUS HUXLEY

JUST AS MUSIC IS
NOISE THAT MAKES SENSE,
A PAINTING IS COLOR
THAT MAKES SENSE, SO
A STORY IS LIFE THAT
MAKES SENSE.

YANN MARTEL

Art enables us to find ourselves and lose ourselves at the same time.

THOMAS MERTON

YOU NEVER HAVE TO
CHANGE ANYTHING YOU
GOT UP IN THE MIDDLE
OF THE NIGHT TO WRITE.

SAUL BELLOW

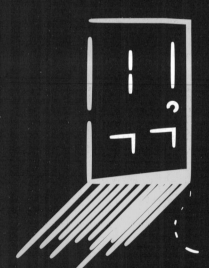

I PICK UP MY PEN.
IT FLOWS. A BUILDING
APPEARS. THERE IT IS.
THERE IS NOTHING
MORE TO SAY.

OSCAR NIEMEYER

Without the magic there is
no art.

Without art there is
no idealism.

Without idealism there is
no integrity.

Without integrity there is
nothing but production.

RAYMOND CHANDLER

In the haunted house of life, art is the only stair that doesn't creak.

TOM ROBBINS

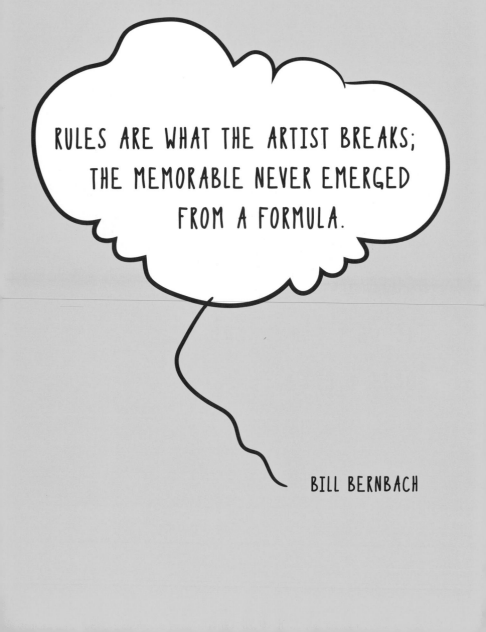

Certainty is a closing of the mind.

To create the new requires doubt.

MILTON GLASER

Any fool can make soap.

It takes a clever man to sell it.

THOMAS J. BARRATT

ANY DAMN FOOL CAN BEG

UP SOME KIND OF JOB;

IT TAKES A WISE MAN TO

MAKE IT WITHOUT WORKING.

CHARLES BUKOWSKI

Genius gives birth, talent delivers. What Rembrandt or Van Gogh saw in the night can never be seen again.

JACK KEROUAC

IT TOOK ME A FEW SECONDS
TO DRAW IT, BUT IT TOOK ME
THIRTY-FOUR YEARS TO LEARN
HOW TO DRAW IT IN A FEW
SECONDS.

PAULA SCHER

Bad design is
smoke, while
good design is
a mirror.

JUAN-CARLOS FERNÁNDEZ

A CLEVER PERSON SOLVES A PROBLEM.
A WISE PERSON AVOIDS IT.

ALBERT EINSTEIN

If a nation loses its storytellers, it loses its childhood.

PETER HANDKE

"Treat a work of art like a prince: Let it speak to you first."

ARTHUR SCHOPENHAUER

A room
without books
is like a body
without a soul.

MARCUS TULLIUS CICERO

NEVER TRUST ANYONE
WHO HAS NOT BROUGHT
A BOOK WITH THEM.

DANIEL HANDLER

Do one thing
every day that
scares you.

MARY SCHMICH

DON'T PANIC.

DOUGLAS ADAMS

"The difference between a brave man and a coward is a coward thinks twice before jumping in the cage with a lion. The brave man doesn't know what a lion is. He just thinks he does."

CHARLES BUKOWSKI

" YES: I AM A DREAMER.
FOR A DREAMER IS ONE WHO
CAN ONLY FIND HIS WAY BY
MOONLIGHT, AND HIS PUNISHMENT
IS THAT HE SEES THE DAWN
BEFORE THE REST OF THE WORLD. **"**

OSCAR WILDE

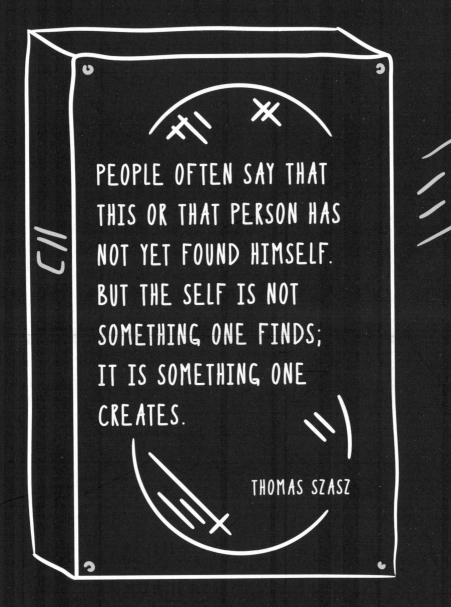

PEOPLE OFTEN SAY THAT
THIS OR THAT PERSON HAS
NOT YET FOUND HIMSELF.
BUT THE SELF IS NOT
SOMETHING ONE FINDS;
IT IS SOMETHING ONE
CREATES.

THOMAS SZASZ

If you ask me what
I came to do in this
world, I, an artist,
will answer you:

I am here to
live out loud.

ÉMILE ZOLA

WE ARE WHAT WE
PRETEND TO BE,

SO WE MUST BE
CAREFUL ABOUT
WHAT WE PRETEND
TO BE.

KURT VONNEGUT

There is no sun
without shadow,
and it is essential to
know the night.

ALBERT CAMUS

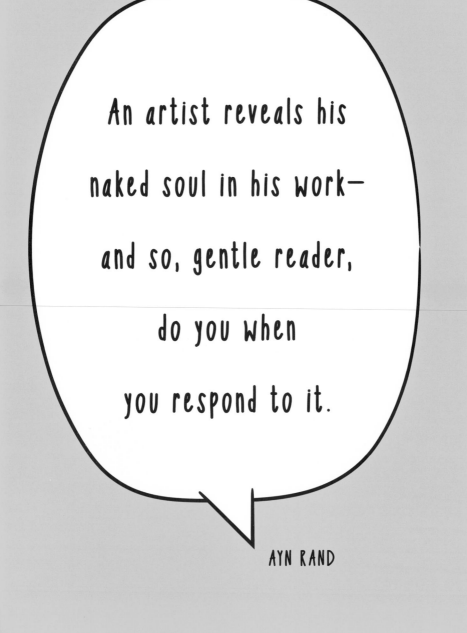

You piss off a bard, and forget about putting a curse on you, he might put a satire on you.

ALAN MOORE

"PRACTICING AN ART, NO MATTER HOW
WELL OR BADLY, IS A WAY TO MAKE
YOUR SOUL GROW, FOR HEAVEN'S SAKE.

SING IN THE SHOWER.

DANCE TO THE RADIO.

TELL STORIES.

WRITE A POEM TO A FRIEND,
         EVEN A LOUSY POEM.

DO IT AS WELL AS YOU POSSIBLY CAN.

YOU WILL GET AN ENORMOUS REWARD. "
YOU WILL HAVE CREATED SOMETHING.

KURT VONNEGUT

Art is anything
you can get
away with.

MARSHALL MCLUHAN

Spec =

ASKING THE WORLD TO
HAVE SEX WITH YOU AND
PROMISING A DINNER DATE
TO ONE LUCKY WINNER.

JEFFREY ZELDMAN

Eroticize intelligence.

DOUGLAS COUPLAND

TRYING TO DEFINE
YOURSELF IS LIKE
TRYING TO BITE
YOUR OWN TEETH.

ALAN WATTS

The height of
originality is skill in
concealing origins.

C.E.M. JOAD

If I got rid of
my demons,
I'd lose my angels.

TENNESSEE WILLIAMS

The height of
originality is skill in
concealing origins.

C.E.M. JOAD

If I got rid of
my demons,
I'd lose my angels.

TENNESSEE WILLIAMS

HEAVEN HAS THE BETTER CLIMATE,
BUT HELL HAS THE BETTER COMPANY.

BEN WADE

"IF I LOSE THE LIGHT OF THE SUN,
I WILL WRITE BY CANDLELIGHT,
MOONLIGHT, NO LIGHT.

IF I LOSE PAPER AND INK,
I WILL WRITE IN BLOOD ON
FORGOTTEN WALLS.

I WILL WRITE ALWAYS. I WILL
CAPTURE NIGHTS ALL OVER THE
WORLD AND BRING THEM TO YOU."

HENRY ROLLINS

Never let the
blood show.

CHARLES EAMES

A photograph is a
secret about a secret.
The more it tells you
the less you know.

DIANE ARBUS

ALL WORTHY WORK IS OPEN TO
INTERPRETATIONS THE AUTHOR DID NOT
INTEND. ART ISN'T YOUR PET—IT'S YOUR KID.
IT GROWS UP AND TALKS BACK TO YOU.

JOSS WHEDON

Drawing is
not what you
see but what
you must make
others see.

EDGAR DEGAS

" PAINTING IS POETRY
THAT IS SEEN RATHER THAN FELT,

AND POETRY IS PAINTING
THAT IS FELT RATHER THAN SEEN. "

LEONARDO DA VINCI

MAKING PEOPLE BELIEVE
THE UNBELIEVABLE IS NO
TRICK; IT'S WORK.

. . . BELIEF AND READER
ABSORPTION COME IN THE
DETAILS: AN OVERTURNED
TRICYCLE IN THE GUTTER
OF AN ABANDONED
NEIGHBORHOOD CAN STAND
FOR EVERYTHING.

STEPHEN KING

IT IS EASIER TO
RECOGNIZE FAILURES OF
TECHNIQUE THAN THOSE
OF STRATEGY OR PURPOSE,
AND SIMPLER TO ASK
"HOW DO I PAINT THIS
TREE?" THAN TO ANSWER
"WHY DOES THIS PAINTING
NEED A TREE IN IT?"

FRANK CHIMERO

Consistency is the last refuge of the unimaginative.

OSCAR WILDE

I DO NOT OVER-INTELLECTUALIZE
THE PRODUCTION PROCESS.
I TRY TO KEEP IT SIMPLE:
TELL THE DAMNED STORY.

TOM CLANCY

WE ARE NOT OUR
BUSINESS CARDS.

WE ARE NOT OUR
RESUMES.

JEFF GREENSPAN

Death to
inspirational
quotes.

GEMMA O'BRIEN

The role of the artist
is to ask questions,
not answer them.

ANTON CHEKHOV

I THINK THE DEEPER YOU GO
INTO QUESTIONS, THE DEEPER
OR MORE INTERESTING THE
QUESTIONS GET.

AND I THINK THAT'S THE
JOB OF ART.

ANDRE DUBUS III

"THE ONLY
DIFFERENCE
BETWEEN A
FLOWER AND
A WEED IS
JUDGMENT."

WAYNE W. DYER

Don't try to win over the haters;

you're not the jackass whisperer.

SCOTT STRATTEN

MANY OF LIFE'S
FAILURES ARE PEOPLE
WHO DID NOT REALIZE
HOW CLOSE THEY WERE
TO SUCCESS WHEN
THEY GAVE UP.

THOMAS EDISON

FAILURE IS THE
CONDIMENT THAT
GIVES SUCCESS
ITS FLAVOR.

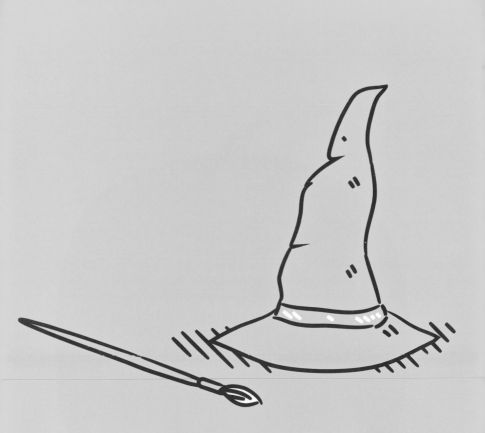

I don't distinguish
between magic and art.

ALAN MOORE

SILENCE IS JUST AS LIKELY TO
INDICATE THE MOST PROFOUND
IDEAS FORMING, THE DEEPEST
ENERGIES BEING SUMMONED.

KAZUO ISHIGURO

WE ARE
UNUSUAL
AND
TRAGIC
AND
ALIVE.

DAVE EGGERS

We all die.

THE GOAL ISN'T TO LIVE FOREVER,
THE GOAL IS TO CREATE SOMETHING
THAT WILL.

CHUCK PALAHNIUK

We write to taste life twice, in the moment, and in retrospection.

ANAÏS NIN

IT IS NOT TRUE THAT PEOPLE
STOP PURSUING DREAMS
BECAUSE THEY GROW OLD,
THEY GROW OLD BECAUSE
THEY STOP PURSUING DREAMS.

GABRIEL GARCÍA MÁRQUEZ

'FORM FOLLOWS PROFIT'
IS THE AESTHETIC
PRINCIPLE OF OUR TIMES.

RICHARD ROGERS

The easier a
thing is to write
then the more the
writer gets paid
for writing it.

(And vice versa:
ask the poets at
the bus stop.)

MARTIN AMIS

Creativity is
not an answer,
it's a process.

STEFAN MUMAW

AN IDEA CAN TURN TO DUST
OR MAGIC DEPENDING ON THE
TALENT THAT RUBS AGAINST IT.

BILL BERNBACH

" Color is my
day-long
obsession,
joy and
torment. "

CLAUDE MONET

COLOR IS THE

TOUCH OF THE EYE,

MUSIC TO THE DEAF,

A WORD OUT OF THE

DARKNESS.

ORHAN PAMUK

IF CATS LOOKED LIKE FROGS WE'D
REALIZE WHAT NASTY, CRUEL LITTLE
BASTARDS THEY ARE.

STYLE. THAT'S WHAT PEOPLE REMEMBER.

TERRY PRATCHETT

Style makes you feel
great because it
takes your mind off
the fact that you're
going to die.

ISAAC MIZRAHI

"A book is really like a lover.

IT ARRANGES ITSELF
IN YOUR LIFE IN A
WAY THAT IS BEAUTIFUL."

MAURICE SENDAK

A book cover is a distillation.
It is a haiku, if you will, of
the story.

CHIP KIDD

IMAGINATION WILL OFTEN CARRY
US TO WORLDS THAT NEVER WERE.

But without it
we go nowhere.

CARL SAGAN

WHO WANTS TO BECOME A WRITER?
AND WHY? BECAUSE IT'S THE
ANSWER TO EVERYTHING. . . .

IT'S THE STREAMING REASON FOR
LIVING. TO NOTE, TO PIN DOWN,
TO BUILD UP, TO CREATE, TO BE
ASTONISHED AT NOTHING, TO CHERISH
THE ODDITIES, TO LET NOTHING GO
DOWN THE DRAIN, TO MAKE SOMETHING,
TO MAKE A GREAT FLOWER OUT OF
LIFE, EVEN IF IT'S A CACTUS.

ENID BAGNOLD

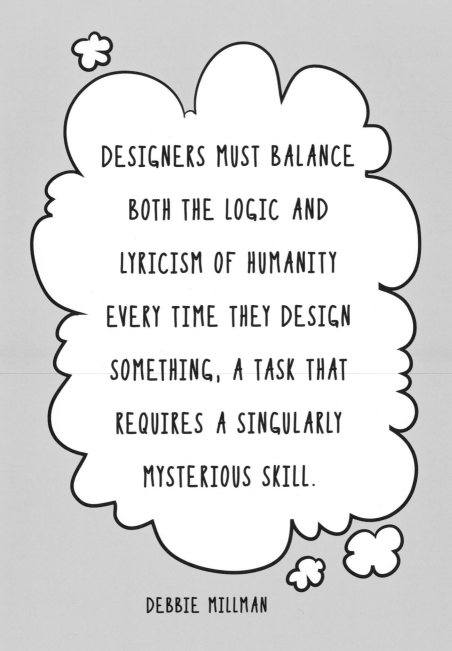

DESIGNERS MUST BALANCE BOTH THE LOGIC AND LYRICISM OF HUMANITY EVERY TIME THEY DESIGN SOMETHING, A TASK THAT REQUIRES A SINGULARLY MYSTERIOUS SKILL.

DEBBIE MILLMAN

" Music expresses
that which cannot
be put into words
and that which
cannot remain
silent. "

VICTOR HUGO

It is amazing how complete is the delusion that beauty is goodness.

LEO TOLSTOY

REMEMBER THAT THE MOST
BEAUTIFUL THINGS IN THE
WORLD ARE THE MOST USELESS;
PEACOCKS AND LILIES, FOR INSTANCE.

JOHN RUSKIN

"All God does is watch us and kill us when we get boring.

We must never, ever be boring."

CHUCK PALAHNIUK

" WHEN THE GOING GETS WEIRD,
THE WEIRD TURN PRO. "

HUNTER S. THOMPSON

AND ONCE THE STORM IS OVER YOU WON'T
REMEMBER HOW YOU MADE IT THROUGH,
HOW YOU MANAGED TO SURVIVE.

YOU WON'T EVEN BE SURE, IN FACT,
WHETHER THE STORM IS REALLY OVER.

BUT ONE THING IS CERTAIN.

WHEN YOU COME OUT OF THE STORM
YOU WON'T BE THE SAME PERSON WHO
WALKED IN. THAT'S WHAT THIS STORM'S
ALL ABOUT.

HARUKI MURAKAMI

WHAT I FEEL FORTUNATE ABOUT IS THAT I'M STILL ASTONISHED, THAT THINGS STILL AMAZE ME.

AND I THINK THAT THAT'S THE GREAT BENEFIT OF BEING IN THE ARTS, WHERE THE POSSIBILITY FOR LEARNING NEVER DISAPPEARS, WHERE YOU BASICALLY HAVE TO ADMIT YOU NEVER LEARN IT.

MILTON GLASER

WE ARE JUST AN ADVANCED
BREED OF MONKEYS ON A MINOR
PLANET OF A VERY AVERAGE STAR.
BUT WE CAN UNDERSTAND THE
UNIVERSE. THAT MAKES US
SOMETHING VERY SPECIAL.

STEPHEN HAWKING

He who wonders
discovers that this in
itself is wonder.

M.C. ESCHER

"The creative
adult is the child
who has survived."

URSULA K. LE GUIN

" Tell me,
what is it you
plan to do with
your one wild
and precious life? "

MARY OLIVER

A NOTE ON ACCURACY

Quotation, n. *The act of repeating erroneously the words of another.*

—Ambrose Bierce, *The Unabridged Devil's Dictionary*

If you want to fact check a quote, you must first uninvent the Internet. Really: It's a quagmire. At some point, people figured out that "quotes about . . ." is one hell of a strong search term, leading to the birth of the online inspiration mill and the death of any semblance of accuracy. (Though, as we might learn from Bierce and *The Devil's Dictionary*, which was published in 1911, the problem has been omnipresent through the halls of history. Technology aside, one misattribution can sour a quote for generations to come.)

Thankfully, certain champions have arisen to fight the good fight and destroy the misattribution blight, and prove to the larger world that Mark Twain and Oscar Wilde, while delightfully quippy and included in this book, did in fact not utter every single clever thought attributed to them on the Internet today.

From among these champions, of particular note are Garson O'Toole and his thank-god-it-exists website Quote Investigator (www.quoteinvestigator.com), and the skilled volunteers at Wikiquote (really!), who maintain an admirable degree of rigorous citation standards, especially in comparison to their faster-and-looser brethren at Wikipedia.

I have made every obsessive effort to present a collection of accurate quotations, not only by digging (and at times slogging) through old journals and books, collections of aphorisms, and lost issues of magazines, but also by conducting interviews.

Moreover, I should note that when I have quoted phrases uttered by fictional characters, I have attributed the words solely to the actual author whose mind spawned the words, despite the ire I know this will inspire in quote purists. I did so in the interest of supplying the designers who worked on this book with a minimal amount of text (and thus fewer constraints), but more importantly with the intention that readers focus more fully on the power of the phrases themselves, which, it is my hope, indeed speak for themselves.

ABOUT THE CURATOR

ZACHARY PETIT is editor-in-chief of the National Magazine Award–winning publication *Print*, author of *The Essential Guide to Freelance Writing: How to Write, Work, and Thrive on Your Own Terms*, and a lifelong literary and design nerd. Formerly, he was the senior managing editor of *HOW* magazine, *Print*, and *Writer's Digest*, and executive editor of several related newsstand titles.

Alongside the thousands of articles he has penned as a staff writer and editor, covering everything from the secret lives of mall Santas to creative legends, his words regularly appear in *National Geographic Kids*, and have also popped up in the pages of *National Geographic*, *Mental_Floss*, *McSweeney's Internet Tendency*, and many other outlets. Give him a shout at www.zacharypetit.com, or on Twitter: @zacharypetit.